RESOLVING CONFLICTS ON THE JOB

SECOND EDITION

RESOLVING CONFLICTS ON THE JOB

SECOND EDITION

Bill Withers
and Jerry Wisinski

AMACOM

American Management Association

New York • Atlanta • Brussels • Chicago • Mexico City • San Francisco
Shanghai • Tokyo • Toronto • Washington, D.C.

This publication is designed to provide accurate and authoritative information in regard to the subject matter covered. It is sold with the understanding that the publisher is not engaged in rendering legal, accounting, or other professional service. If legal advice or other expert assistance is required, the services of a competent professional person should be sought.

Library of Congress Cataloging-in-Publication Data

Withers, Bill.
    Resolving conflicts on the job / Bill Withers and Jerry Wisinski.—2nd ed.
        p.   cm.
    Includes index.
    ISBN-13: 978-0-8144-7413-6 (pbk.)
    ISBN-10: 0-8144-7413-6 (pbk.)
    1. Conflict management.   I. Wisinski, Jerry.   II. Title.

HD42.W573   2007
658.4'053—dc22

                                                              2007007078

Printing number

10   9   8   7   6   5   4   3   2   1

To Julia

CONTENTS

PREFACE TO THE SECOND EDITION

―――――――

Telling people how to think about conflict makes about as much sense as teaching dogs how to think about eating. By the time we are adults, we know a lot about conflict and know what we think about it. We face conflict every day—as we struggle within ourselves, and as we interact with family, friends, coworkers, and the rest of our world.

As adults, we have organized what we have learned about conflict into our own personal theories. We know what conflict is and where it comes from, what we think about it, and how we go about it. We know what works for us, and what doesn't. We know when we should adhere to our theory and when we should try something else. We know when we are trying something else because we think it is good for us, and when we are trying something else because we are backsliding.

When I spend time with groups of adults who come to workshops to learn about conflict, I tell them that they are a "room full of experts." They have all organized their experience into a set of rules for what to do when—their personal theories of conflict. The only reason for these experts to come together is to compare notes or to learn about other people's approaches. As the teacher, I may have spent more time reading, thinking about, and consciously observing conflict than they have. I may be able to share some theories about conflict that are different from the ones they have crafted. They get a chance to try some ideas on for size, compare notes with the other experts in the room, and just maybe come away with some new actions to apply to their daily lives.

In these workshops, we always leave room for "f'rinstances." This is a half hour or more at the end of the workshop when participants can ask about specific applications: "F'rinstance, there's this guy at work. . . ." Nine times out of ten the person posing the case knows just what needs to be done and wants to hear from me or the group that there is some easier way or wants reassurance that he or she can act without risk. Sometimes, though, the person will come up with something entirely new—a different way of seeing the conflict, a different way to act, a different way to react, or a different way to think or feel.

This is when real learning takes place.

In the first edition of this book, Jerry Wisinski created a similar pattern for learning—that is, the chapters have some ideas for you to think about that are followed by exercises to help you reflect on what you are learning and to see if you can apply this knowledge to your life. We have updated some language in this new edition to reflect advances in the field since 1993, and we added some new things to think about that I have culled from my experience as a mediator and a teacher, and from my work with people at all levels of businesses and nonprofit organizations. A new chapter on giving and receiving feedback will be helpful to people who dread that infamous management task. The chapter on teamwork has been updated, and there are new tools for reflecting on conflict and to help you to analyze specific conflicts you are working through and for planning how you can best approach another person at work with whom you may be having a difference.

The appendix at the end of the book pulls many of the reflective questions together to help you to remember what you have learned and to apply it to your own real-world situation.

As you read, think of your own "f'rinstances" and use those to work through the exercises. The exercises are simple, and if you only read through them, you will find nothing helpful in them. If, instead, you write out your answers and use the exercises to help you to think through your own "f'rinstances," you may be surprised to learn what a conflict expert you really are.

ACKNOWLEDGMENTS

The exercises in this book are meant for you to perform alone as reflection pieces. Some are based on training exercises for groups introduced in my book *The Conflict Management Skills Workshop* and in *The Conflict and Communication Activity Book*, which I wrote with Keami D. Lewis. I am grateful to Keami for her help in clarifying, testing, and reporting those exercises.

The many people who have contributed to my thinking by participating in workshops and seminars, and especially those who have honored me by allowing me to work with them as a mediator, continue to help me by sharing their own expertise and experience. Thanks to all of you for being my best teachers.

Bill Withers

January 2007
Ellicott City, Maryland

RESOLVING CONFLICTS ON THE JOB

SECOND EDITION

A BRIEF OVERVIEW OF CONFLICT

Conflict is a fact of life. Every one of us has been involved in conflict and has survived the experience. We all have some idea, then, of how to deal with conflict. We also all know that a conflict ignored does not go away, and—though we may not look forward to it—we also know that it is preferable to figure out how best to deal with the conflict rather than pretend that it will disappear.

THE POSITIVE VIEW OF CONFLICT

It's easy to think of conflict at work as a bad thing—something to be avoided at all costs. Associated with undesirable behavior, conflict seems to be a characteristic of individuals who can't get along with others, aren't team players, or simply don't fit in. In fact, there are plenty of books and websites that tell us how to work with so-called difficult people.

As you work through the exercises in this book, try to decide what to change about your approaches to conflict in order to make conflict more constructive for you. A good question that I ask myself about difficult people is, "What am I doing that is contributing to making this person difficult?"

MYTHS AND TRUTHS ABOUT CONFLICT

Many of us hold strong negative feelings about conflict. When we start a workshop by asking people to speak briefly about their view of conflict, the vast majority say they hate it or avoid it at all costs. What is easy to forget is that we engage in conflict as part of every human activity. Here are some conflict "myths" and "truths" for you to consider:

Myths

■ *Conflict at work always means that there is something seriously wrong with the company or organization.* Not always. When handled effectively, conflict can help people meet their goals and objectives within your team or department, with other departments, and even throughout your entire organization. Constructive conflict even allows us to create new solutions by incorporating ideas from several points of view.

■ *Conflict means communication has come to a halt.* When we know how to positively engage each other in a conflict, it can provide the opportunity for us to clarify issues, create innovative solutions, and strengthen relationships.

■ *If avoided, conflict will eventually go away.* Not usually. Minor issues may sometimes resolve themselves, but more often than not, conflict needs to be addressed in order to be positive.

■ *All conflicts can be resolved.* That would be nice, wouldn't it? However, because you have different values from others, there will be times when you simply cannot agree on certain issues. So, we make choices about which differences to engage for solutions, which differences to engage for learning, and which differences to leave alone.

■ *Conflict always results in a winner and a loser.* Not true. There are many possible outcomes to a conflict. In fact, when mutual desire exists to resolve the differences, you can increase the chances for a win/win result.

Truths

■ *Conflict* will *occur.* Without question. It is a natural dynamic when interacting with others. The more important question is what you do with conflict when it occurs.

■ *Most conflicts can be managed.* Well, you can't fix everything, and you can't always get what you want. But most, if not all, differences can be engaged in a constructive way. You have at least five options at your disposal: competition, accommodation, avoidance, compromise, and collaboration. Then again, you can always agree to disagree. Most of the time, one of these options will enable you to manage your differences.

■ *Conflict can help build relationships.* This may sound contradictory, but it's true. In attempting to deal with differences that are important to you, it is possible to strengthen relationships with bosses, peers, and employees. When we know how to work with people in conflict situations, we learn about ourselves, our beliefs, and each other.

■ *Conflict can be a tool for personal development.* In the process of addressing differences, we are exposed to new ideas and have the opportunity to reassess our thinking and how we act on it. Take a few minutes and answer the following questions to begin setting the stage for your learning as you work through this book.

1. With whom are you currently experiencing differences at work?

Boss(es)/upper management?

_____

_____

Peers?

_____

_____

Employees?

_____

_____

2. Recently, what conflicts have you handled well?

Describe the conflict:

_____

_____

_____

_____

What did you do?

_____

_____

_____

_____

How did things work out?

_____

_____

_____

_____

Describe the conflict:

_____

_____

_____

_____

What did you do?

_____

_____

_____

_____

How did things work out?

_____

_____

_____

_____

3. What workplace conflicts have you *not* handled well?

Describe the conflict:

_____

_____

_____

_____

What did you do?

_____

_____

_____

_____

How did things work out?

_____

_____

_____

_____

4. What do you think would happen if you approached the person(s) you listed?

Name:

What might you say or do?

_____

_____

_____

_____

What do you think might happen?

_____

_____

_____

_____

Name:

What might you say or do?

_____

_____

_____

_____

What do you think might happen?

_____

_____

_____

_____

If you are unhappy with some of the answers to these questions, use this book to learn more about some of the issues surrounding conflict in the workplace and to learn some tools to help you to address differences as they occur.

CHAPTER II

2

WHY PEOPLE FIGHT AT WORK

We can divide most of what people fight over into three general categories: not enough stuff to go around, goals they want to reach, and different ways of seeing the world. Most often at work, conflicts seem to be about resources, turf boundaries, or conflicting goals. Although these issues may present themselves as the conflict, what we value often plays a big part in how conflicts play themselves out.

Consider the following case studies.

CASE STUDY 1

Mary and Tom are working together on a very important project. The project is on schedule, but just barely. Because they can only work together in the afternoon, Mary suggests staying an hour or so later to gain a little cushion on the deadline. Tom won't hear of it. The way Tom sees it, he puts in a full day's effort and is not about to give up any personal time. Besides, he says, the project is on schedule.

1. What is the potential conflict here?

_____

_____

_____

_____

2. What is Mary's work value regarding the project?

_____

_____

_____

_____

3. What is Tom's work value regarding the project?

_____

_____

_____

_____

Who is right here, Mary or Tom? Can they both be right? Is this one of those times when there is more than one way to see and respond to what is going on?

CASE STUDY 2

As a manager, John has always performed to the utmost of his ability. He is also a true believer in climbing the corporate ladder.

Peggy—who reports to John—meets every one of her performance goals and always receives good reviews. John feels that if Peggy really applied herself, she could do even better and move up in the organization. It frustrates John that Peggy seems to be so involved outside work. She is president of the PTA at her son's school and does a lot of volunteer work in her community.

Because John sees how focused Peggy is at work and outside, he thinks that if she would channel all her energy into her job, she would quickly be promoted. John has tried to explain the potential for growth in the company, but Peggy just doesn't seem interested.

1. What is the potential conflict here?

_____

_____

_____

_____

2. How does John view success?

_____

_____

_____

_____

3. How might Peggy view success?

_____

_____

_____

_____

4. How do you think John should handle this situation?

_____

_____

_____

_____

VALUES

It is common for us to want other people to see things the same way that we do—especially about what we would consider to be core work values such as getting a project finished, balancing work and family, or advancing in our profession. However, we each have our own value system through which we determine our priorities. When different priorities collide, conflict is often the result. How we engage these differences becomes critically important.

The roots of your value system can be traced back to your early childhood, school years, adolescence, early adulthood, and significant events in your adult life. However, how are they developed? Why are yours different from others? How do you know which ones are right? Can your values be changed? These are important questions when examining your values in contrast to the values of other people.

CONFLICTING GOALS AND OBJECTIVES

Sometimes conflict over goals at work is the result of poor communication and planning. The goals and objectives of one department may clash with those of another department.

LIMITED RESOURCES

Limited resources can mean practically anything: not enough employees, lack of space, shortage of finances, outdated equipment, and so on.

THE DOMINO EFFECT

The domino effect is the product of poor planning and communication breakdown. It occurs when the activities of one department have an impact on the activities of another department, the activities of which have an impact on yet another department, and on and on.

Example: The director of sales has promised his employees an all-expenses-paid trip to Hawaii if they increase widget sales by 15 percent over the next quarter. The sales staff is very excited, and sales begin increasing immediately. However, no one has told the production department, which immediately falls behind; or the shipping department, which won't have enough widget boxes if production catches up; or customer service, which will surely become involved when the widgets don't arrive as promised by the salespeople who wanted to go to Hawaii.

How would you address this problem?

_____

_____

_____

_____

How would you keep this problem from happening in the first place?

_____

_____

_____

_____

CHAPTER III

3

FIVE WAYS TO ENGAGE CONFLICT

As stated in Chapter 1, conflict is inevitable. The real issue is how we deal with it. We can't always avoid it, nor can we always resolve it, but we can often engage it in some productive way.

How we tend to view conflict can influence how we react when it happens. We can see conflict as a contest to win, as a problem to solve, or as an opportunity to learn about ourselves and others.

If we see conflict as a contest to win, there have to be winners and losers. Somebody is going to be disappointed. If our contest ends up in a tie, both parties can end up disappointed. If we see conflict as a problem to solve, we analyze the conflict and look for solutions. We can work on these solutions by ourselves and present them to the other side, or we can work with the other side to generate solutions together. If we see conflict as a chance to learn, we can approach it in a completely different way. If we want to learn about the conflict, we need to invite both sides to examine the source of the difference, the source of our thinking about the difference, and be willing to challenge sometimes long-held opinions or conclusions about the difference.

Here are five common methods people use to engage conflict.

COMPETITION (WIN/LOSE)

The competitive, win/lose approach to conflict is an attempt at complete dominance. It is a "winner take all" position. Usually, the focus is on winning the conflict at all costs, rather than on searching for the most appropriate solution for everyone involved.

The win/lose approach is a power-based mode. You use whatever power you think you have available to win people over to your position. If you see conflict as a contest to be won, then your approach to winning that conflict is to use everything you can to defeat the other side, such as rank, influence, alliances, money, and so forth.

ACCOMMODATION (LOSE/WIN)

Accommodation is a variation on the competitive approach. With this method, you are willing to lose the "contest" to the other person. Some of us seem to approach all conflict this way, but accommodation is different from just caving in.

Effective application of the lose/win approach comes from an assertive position. You can actually assertively choose to accommodate for reasons other than timidity or avoidance.

You may choose to accommodate when dealing with the following situations:

■ It is more important to preserve the relationship than to argue the issue.

■ The issue is more important to the other person than it is to you.

■ You want to send a signal to the other side that you are a reasonable person.

■ You want to encourage others to express their own point of view.

■ You want others to learn by their own choices and actions.

AVOIDANCE (LOSE/LOSE)

On the surface, avoiding conflict appears to be inappropriate for resolving differences. Avoidance is often seen as a fear response, an unwillingness to cooperate, or a denial that a problem exists. Avoidance is referred to as the lose/lose outcome because the avoider seems unable to even deal with the issue, much less manage or resolve it.

However, when appropriately applied, avoidance can actually help to resolve differences between two people.

Example: In the heat of an argument when nothing seems to be getting accomplished, temporary avoidance gives each party time to cool off: "Phil, this isn't getting us anywhere. Why don't we give it a rest for a while and discuss it later when we've both calmed down a little?"

When this approach is used, it is important that the person who calls the time-out initiate the issue again within an appropriate amount of time. If this doesn't happen, the temporary avoidance can be perceived as a manipulative move used to simply ignore or to avoid the issue entirely.

You may choose to avoid a particular conflict when faced with the following conditions:

■ Others can resolve the conflict more effectively.

■ The negative impact of the situation itself may be too damaging or costly to both parties involved.

■ Additional time is required.

■ Both parties need a chance to cool off.

COMPROMISE (WIN/LOSE–WIN/LOSE)

Compromise strategies include negotiation, trade-offs, swapping, and a high degree of flexibility. It is referred to as the win/lose–win/lose position because, although you will get some of what you want, you will also have to give up something else in the process.

It is important to decide in advance how much you are willing to give away before you begin to negotiate. In other words, you need to set limits. This doesn't necessarily mean you must give away everything up to that point; setting limits in advance simply gives you a range within which you can negotiate effectively.

When using compromise to resolve differences, you indicate concern not only for your own objectives but also for maintenance of the relationship. Compromise is an attempt to find the common ground of agreement. Both parties win some aspects of the issue while giving up others.

You may choose to compromise in order to accomplish the following:

■ Reach agreement when both sides have equal power

■ Find a common ground when both parties have competing goals

■ Achieve temporary settlement in complex matters

■ Reach a solution under difficult circumstances or time pressures

■ Advance personal objectives while preserving the relationship

COLLABORATION (WIN/WIN)

When people are collaborating, there is a maximum concern both for the issues and for the maintenance of the relationship on both sides. Collaboration requires a climate that will enable each person to examine and understand the other person's point of view. It is referred to as the win/win approach because it involves identifying those areas where agreements exist and where there are differences, evaluating alternatives, and selecting solutions that have the full support and commitment of both parties.

This kind of problem solving requires an atmosphere of trust, the surfacing of hidden agendas, and the willingness to be creative in order to reach resolution. In addition, certain conditions must be agreed upon to achieve the win/win result.

Conditions for Successful Collaboration

■ *Willingness to Resolve.* Both parties *must* be willing to resolve the conflict.

■ *Willingness to Go to the Root Problem.* Often, what appears to be the problem is only a symptom of the real issue. Both parties must be willing to explore the origins of the conflict in order to identify its true source and deal with it.

■ *Willingness to Empathize.* Feelings are always a part of conflict. Both sides need to be willing to understand the other person's feelings and point of view, even though they might not agree with each other. Agreement isn't the issue. The point is to understand and respect the other person's position.

You may choose to collaborate when you want to accomplish the following:

■ Preserve important objectives that can't be compromised while still maintaining the relationship

■ Merge experiences and feelings from people who have different backgrounds and perspectives

■ Create new joint alternatives

■ Get at unresolved root problems that may have hindered the working relationship over a long period of time

The key to using these different approaches to conflict engagement is to choose consciously based upon the conflict and what you would like to have happen.

Think of a conflict at work.

1. What do you want?

_____

_____

_____

_____

2. What is at stake?

_____

_____

_____

_____

3. What approach should you use?

_____

_____

_____

_____

CHAPTER IV

WAYS TO LISTEN

M ost of us think that we are good listeners. Most of us aren't. Listening is not the natural process we think it is because of the time difference between the relatively slow rate of speech and the much faster rate of processing. On average, we speak at approximately 125 to 150 words per minute, depending on the culture we were raised in and where we currently live. For example, if we're from the city, we may tend to talk very fast; if we're from the country, we may tend to talk rather slowly. However, no matter where we're from, our processing rate is four to six times our speaking rate. In short, most of us can process much faster than someone else can talk.

This leaves us with a lot of free time to do other things while the other person is speaking. We drift off, fantasize, or travel down our mind's highway on a mental vacation. Of course, every now and then we check back in by nodding our head, muttering "uh-huh," or "oh, really," or "no kidding?" or whatever. But we're not really *listening*, and we're certainly not responding.

FIVE LEVELS OF ACTIVE LISTENING AND RESPONDING SKILLS

Here is a list of five levels of active listening and responding skills, beginning with the simplest and graduating to the more complex.

Level 1. Basic Acknowledgments

Some of the basic acknowledgments have already been mentioned. Nonverbal responses include head nodding, leaning forward or backward, folding or unfolding arms, making eye contact or looking away, and so on. Verbal responses include saying, "uh-huh," "oh, really," "no kidding?" "nah," "huh?" and so on.

Although these responses are basic, they are nonetheless necessary in letting the speaker know you're listening. Of course, you can use these same responses to take that mental vacation discussed previously. However, the positive intention of these basic acknowledgments is to indicate that you are actively listening to what is being said.

Level 2. Silence

As the saying goes, "Silence is golden." This statement could not be truer than when applied to engaging conflict. However, silence is difficult for most of us. We are conditioned to speak rather than listen. But when we are able to discipline ourselves to be silent, we usually find out more information from the speaker.

When you reach a natural pause in what you're saying, you normally expect the listener to respond to you. If there is silence, you probably have a tendency to add additional information. A good interviewer uses this method when trying to get at information the interviewee may not have originally wanted to reveal.

Silence can also be a powerful opportunity to take time to think or to change the pace of a conversation. Practice stopping to think before speaking. As you become comfortable with silence, you will be less likely to fall victim to the urge to fill it with talk.

Level 3. Questions

The idea of asking questions may seem contradictory at first: How can you be listening if you're asking questions? In fact, asking questions not only tells the speaker that you're interested in what is being said, it also tells the speaker that you want to know more. Asking questions helps to gain a better understanding of the other person's point of view.

Level 4. Paraphrasing

Paraphrasing is a response tool used to verify understanding on the part of the listener. It focuses on content and involves interpreting what you think the speaker has said, then getting verification that you are correct. There are certain steps to take when using the paraphrasing process. They are outlined in the box "Steps for Paraphrasing."

Steps for Paraphrasing

■ *Let the other person finish speaking.* Although this is generally the rule, a courteous interruption is sometimes appropriate. Beginning with a phrase such as, "Excuse me, but let me see if I understand what you're saying," is better than not interrupting and then missing the message.

■ *Restate what you think the other person has said.* The intent here is not to parrot the speaker but to repeat in your own words what you think has been said.

■ *If the speaker confirms your understanding, continue the conversation.*

■ *If the speaker indicates that you have misunderstood what has been said, then ask the speaker to repeat.* When attempting to resolve differences, how you handle your misunderstandings is important. If you tell someone, "You're not making yourself clear . . . ," you may sound accusatory and perhaps intensify the situation. Conversely, if you say, "I'm not understanding you; could you say that again?" you are choosing more neutral language while asking for clarification.

There is one caution when using paraphrasing: Don't overuse it. You can always tell when someone has just completed a course in listening skills. After passing the person in the hallway, you nod and say, "Good morning, how are you doing?" If the person stops you and says, "Excuse me, let me see if I understand what you're saying . . . ," he or she has just been to a seminar and is in the midst of paraphrasing everything.

Paraphrasing should be used in order to:

1. Summarize

2. Clarify a critical thought

3. Confirm your understanding

It is not intended to be used in superficial conversations.

Level 5. Reflective Listening

As stated previously, paraphrasing focuses on clarity of content. In contrast, reflective listening focuses on responding to the speaker's emotion.

How you phrase your statements is critical. If you are emotionally involved, it is very easy to sound accusatory rather than concerned.

Here are some examples of reflective listening:

Accusatory Reflective Statements

■ "Well, look at this, you're [emotion]."

■ "Go ahead, feel [emotion]."

■ "I knew you would react like a(an) [emotion] person."

Concerned Reflective Statements

■ "You seem [emotion] about this."

■ "I'm concerned about your [emotion]."

■ "I think you're feeling [emotion] right now."

The real value of reflective listening is that it tells the speaker you are working to understand not only what he or she is saying but also how he or she feels about it.

1. Who is the best listener you know?

_____

2. What specifically does this person do when listening?

_____

_____

_____

_____

3. How would others rate you as a listener? What levels do you currently use? Which do you need to develop?

_____

_____

_____

_____

LISTENING AND RESPONDING
TO THE EXCESSIVE TALKER

It is important to remember that what is excessive talking for one person may be just the right amount of information or enthusiasm for another. Many people are most comfortable processing information by thinking aloud. To a person who talks little and moves quickly to conclusions, this seems like far too much talk. To another person whose brain works the same way, it may seem perfectly normal.

Listening and responding to the excessive talker is difficult, but it is not impossible. However, you must actively engage in the conversation to get the information you need presented in the way that you need it. There are two tools you can use to do this.

1. *Interrupting.* As a child, you were probably taught not to interrupt, but you can use interrupting to better participate in the conversation. Phrases such as "Excuse me, but . . ." or "Let me see if I understand you . . ." allow us to break into the conversation and ask for specific information without putting the speaker on the defensive.

Some people who talk a lot also interrupt a lot. Interrupting may very well be a part of their everyday approach to conversation. A good way to check is to interrupt and see if they mind.

2. *Focusing.* In effect, focusing is asking the speaker to come to the point. A simple phrase such as "So, your point is . . ." or "Then the bottom line is . . ." will usually help put the conversation back on track.

Depending on your relationship with the speaker, perhaps you could tactfully let the speaker know that you would like to work on how you exchange information. Give an example of what will work for you, see what the other person prefers, and be willing to compromise. We run the risk of hurting feelings or perhaps causing temporary conflict, but it may help in the long run, making it worth the effort.

How well you listen can be a strong signal to others about how valuable you consider their ideas and feelings to be.

Think of a conflict you were involved in that you wish you could do over.

1. How well did you listen?

_____

_____

_____

_____

2. What would you do differently?

_____

_____

_____

_____

3. Think of a conflict you were involved in that you feel you handled well.

_____

_____

_____

_____

4. What listening approach(es) did you use?

_____

_____

_____

_____

5. What will you do next time?

_____

_____

_____

_____

CHAPTER V

5

WAYS TO GIVE (AND RECEIVE) FEEDBACK

W e all want to be able to tell other people what we think of them without getting into trouble. The following seven rules for feedback can help us do this.

SEVEN RULES OF GIVING FEEDBACK

Most of us think that we can usually accept constructive criticism if it is delivered the right way. But what is the right way? If you are giving someone feedback at work that wasn't asked for, chances are you are the boss. This leads us to our first rule of giving feedback.

1. Use Authority Lightly

If you are in charge, the person you are talking to knows it. There is no need to constantly remind him or her of this fact. For many of us, receiving any communication from someone in charge makes us instantly defensive. See what you can do to downplay the differences in position.

The second rule of giving feedback will help you with this goal.

2. Choose the Setting Well

If the communication is important enough to have, then choose a setting where it will be easiest to hear. Important feedback should not be delivered when passing in the hallway or on the elevator, on a noisy shop floor, or in front of a lot of people. If you are in your office, can you set the furniture up to minimize the intimidation factor? Coming around the desk and sitting next to the person can go a long way to reducing some of the tension caused by having to talk with the boss.

3. Arrange the Feedback in Advance

Just as designing the setting is important, so is choosing the time. Nobody likes to be ambushed. A good approach is to let the person know that you will be talking about whatever the issue is in advance. A better approach is to schedule the feedback when you schedule the expectation: "We'll meet every Thursday at 3:00 to go over your progress on this project."

Of course, in order to do that, you need to follow the fourth rule of giving feedback.

4. No Surprises

If there are no surprises, then why does the person need feedback? "No surprises" means that clear and specific expectations were set in advance of the feedback session. You have agreed not only to what is expected but also that the feedback will be at a certain time, in a certain structure, and about specific items.

5. Be Specific

People listen better to feedback when it is clear and concise. If the feedback is about job performance, pick one item to talk about. Try the following format for your feedback:

"We agreed that you would complete _____ by _____. At this point, you have done _____. We need to _____."

If the feedback is about some behavior that has upset you, be sure that you are calm and then try this format:

"When you do _____, it makes me feel _____. I need you to do _____ instead."

There is nothing fancy about these statements. In fact, you want to avoid fancy. Stick to facts as you see them, avoid personal attacks, say your one or two sentences, then be quiet and follow rule number six.

6. Listen

If you stop at rule five, you will have given feedback. If you want the feedback to be heard—and if you want future feedback sessions to go well—you need to speak your piece, ask, "What ideas do you have?" and then be quiet and listen. If you ask the question honestly and are open to alternatives, you may discover new ways to improve the situation.

In order to do this, you need to be willing to listen to feedback from other people. One way to make this easier for you is to agree on the approach to giving and getting feedback with the other person. Share this chapter with people with whom you need to exchange feedback. Stick to the script, forgive yourself and each other if you make mistakes while you are learning, and take some time to follow rule number seven.

7. Check In

Two other questions you are allowed to ask while still keeping feedback simple are, "How did I do?" and "Do you understand?" Checking in with the other person who is giving you feedback or getting it from you is the best way to find out if you are having the effect you desire. Ask these questions and then see rule number six.

WHAT IF THE PERSON GETS MAD ANYWAY?

Of course, sometimes we still get upset when people give us feedback. Knowing how to handle other people's anger or frustration is an important skill when giving feedback. Even our best efforts can be answered with anger, and it is nearly impossible to settle differences when emotions are in the way. However, there is a two-step method for dealing with this type of situation.

The Two-Step Method for Dealing with Anger

1. *Allow the person to express the emotion.* As mentioned previously, it is nearly impossible to resolve an issue when emotions are in the way. Therefore, your first step is to allow the person to express her or his emotion. It is important not to take things personally when attempting this first step.

Using statements like, "I can see you're upset," or "I can understand that you're angry," should help in this step. Although these statements indicate empathy, they do not necessarily indicate agreement.

2. *Deal with the content.* After the individual has released his or her anger, you can begin to address the reasons for that feeling. Apologize if you have done something you should apologize for doing. Remind the person of whatever performance or actions you had previously agreed to, solicit ideas for improvement, and listen. Generate solutions together, including a plan for what to do the next time feedback is delivered.

PREPARING FOR YOUR FEEDBACK SESSION

As you will see in Chapter 7, it is not usually helpful to overstrategize when you want to talk someone. It can help, though, to organize your thinking before starting a difficult conversation. Here are some questions to think about before your feedback session.

You may be the nicest person in the world, but if you're the boss, it is still a little scary to get feedback from you. What can you do to help the other person feel less threatened before, during, and after your feedback session?

Where should you have this conversation? What effect might your choice of setting have on your attitude and on the other person's attitude?

What can you do to set the stage in advance? Can you e-mail an agenda? Schedule regular sessions for feedback? Ensure that all expectations are very clear?

How can you be sure that your feedback is specific? What is the topic that you need to cover? What clear examples can you give to illustrate successes and shortcomings? What behavior would you like to see going forward? How will you follow up?

CHAPTER VI

CONFLICT STYLES

Many books written about conflict discuss various conflict styles, based on the idea that we each have a dominant way of engaging in conflict. Experience shows us, though, that each of us can use any of these styles and that we choose to use the one that we think will work best. Sometimes, the choice may be unconscious or the result of habit—for example, we always act a certain way when arguing with our sister.

So, no matter our personalities, we shift our approach to conflict and may make poor choices. Knowing some of the approaches will help us to make effective choices.

Four commonly recognized conflict behaviors are:

1. Aggressive

2. Nonassertive

3. Passive-aggressive

4. Assertive

In considering the profiles of these styles, you can examine the thought process, actions, verbal cues, and how we are responding to conflict when we choose a particular style. In the following profiles, consider several differences you have been involved in recently. See what you can learn about your conflict behavior by checking off different behaviors you have used. Think about what worked best when it comes to preserving and improving positive working relationships.

AGGRESSIVE BEHAVIOR

Pure aggression aims at preserving our rights while attempting to take away the rights of others.

Expressed Attitudes

■ "I have rights, but you don't."

■ "My feelings are more important than yours are."

■ "I am never wrong."

■ "People should do what I tell them to do."

■ "Don't argue with me."

Verbal Cues

■ "You must . . ."

■ "Because I said so . . ."

■ "You dummy . . ."

■ "I'm warning you . . ."

We choose aggression when we know we can dominate a person or situation. Sometimes we think of it as a shortcut and make excuses that justify the behavior.

When we use aggression this way, it is often because we feel that we must win at all costs. Sometimes the issue may fade in importance as the conflict unfolds, and the need to win becomes the driving force. We may use intimidation, misuse a position of authority, threaten, or personally attack the individual, rather than attempt to find the best outcome for the situation. This extreme win/lose approach may save time, but the cost can be very high.

NONASSERTIVE BEHAVIOR

Sometimes we cave in to keep the peace or to get a situation over with. This approach also carries a price to be paid later.

Expressed Attitudes

■ "I must be nice."

■ "Don't make waves. If you do, you won't be liked."

■ "Others have rights, but I don't."

■ "I'm not worthy."

Verbal Cues

- "I can't . . ."
- "I wish . . ."
- "If only I could . . ."
- "I'll never be able to . . ."
- "I probably should . . ."

We use nonassertive behavior when we get cold feet at having to face a difficult matter, don't like saying no for fear of causing hard feelings, or are having a very difficult time making decisions. People using this style may agree externally, while at the same time disagreeing internally. Often, they expect you to guess what they want or what is wrong.

Unintentional Gunnysacking

When we approach conflict nonassertively, we are unintentionally "gunnysacking." That is, we gather grievances over a period of time without responding to them when they occur. We figure that "It's no big deal" or "That's okay, I can go along. . . ." But the gunnysack fills, and we become less able to swallow our feelings. At some point, we explode, aggressively dumping the collected grievances on whoever happens to be around. This action is often surprising to us and to whoever is on the receiving end for two reasons:

1. What caused us to explode often doesn't seem to be a big deal.
2. Our switch to aggression is completely beyond what we and others would expect from us.

PASSIVE-AGGRESSIVE BEHAVIOR

Passive aggression is a combination of aggression and nonassertive behavior. At first, this style is nonconfrontational, signaling nonassertiveness. Some of us use passive aggression more than others, but we are all guilty when we pretend to let a conflict slide but intend to "fix" it later.

Expressed Attitudes

- "I'll pay you now, but you'll pay me later."
- "Subtle sabotage pays off."
- "Better to be cunning than confrontational."
- "Never show your cards."
- "Don't let them know what you're planning."

Verbal Cues

- "Well, if that's the way you want it . . ."
- "I told you so . . ."
- "How could you even think that is what I meant?"
- "Everyone knows that I was kidding."
- "Who . . . me?"

We are often surprised if someone points out that we are being passive-aggressive. Often, we started out being accommodating or avoiding the conflict altogether, then switched to aggression when we became fed up or decided that maybe we could "win."

The best way to address passive aggression is to point it out. Try this format: "You had indicated before that this didn't matter to you, and now it does. Is something different from before, or should we start from where we began?" If you are caught or catch yourself being passive-aggressive, ask yourself the same question. It could be that something you thought you could sacrifice is more important to you than you thought.

Intentional Gunnysacking

If someone uses passive aggression as a consciously chosen strategy, then he or she "gunnysacks," but with a difference. This person may start out by being accommodating (passive) but will also collect any and all items that could be used against someone at a later date. It is at this point that the aggressive side surfaces, resulting in a gotcha! outcome.

When we use passive aggression as a strategy, we may score some short-term wins, but we pay the long-term price of lost trust.

ASSERTIVE BEHAVIOR

Being assertive is a way to engage in conflict by standing your ground while being respectful of others. We get better at this approach with practice and by reminding ourselves of how we want to behave before and during conflict situations.

Expressed Attitudes

- "I have rights and so do others."
- "People deserve my respect."
- "I may not always win, but I can always manage the situation."
- "It is best to deal with issues as they occur."
- "Mistakes can be corrected."

Verbal Cues

- "What are our options?"
- "You're right, it's my mistake."
- "What can we do to . . . ?"
- "I choose to . . ."
- "What are the real issues here?"

HANDLING CONFLICT

As we build our assertive behavior skills, we become better at effectively engaging conflict. We choose the approach to conflict that will benefit everyone, without causing harm to ourselves. The ideal is to attempt collaboration (win/win) with the other person. Of course, this is the most difficult result to achieve, so the assertive person is prepared for compromise when necessary. In addition, choosing this behavioral style indicates that we are also capable of accommodation when the issue's relative importance to the other party can be determined.

Take a look at the checkmarks you made about your conflict choices as you read this chapter. How did you do? Is there a style that you use more than others? Are there situations or people that lead you to choosing a particular style? Are you happy with your choices?

CHAPTER VII

7

STAYING COOL IN A CONFLICT

M any people attend workshops on conflict because they want to know how to stay calm when someone else is being highly emotional. They often say, "I know what I'm supposed to say, but I have trouble staying calm enough to do the right thing. By the time I thought of what I should have said, I was at home, had dinner, and was lying in bed looking at the ceiling." (This chapter is adapted from workshops run by Bill Withers and Keami Lewis as reported in their book *The Conflict and Communication Activity Book.*)

Some people seem to be better than others when it comes to knowing what to say and do under pressure. These individuals come across as unflappable, in control, maybe even wise. How do they do it?

There are many things that may help people stay unruffled in a conflict. One is that they have a lot of practice being in conflict situations. Another is that they feel reasonably sure that things will work out the way they want them to. A third way is that they are not upset because they have decided not to be upset.

Practice counts for a lot. Exercises like the ones in this book can help even very inexperienced people to invent new ways to respond to conflict. The more practice we have—in practice scenarios and in real life—the more nimble we are when a conflict seems to be about to boil over.

HOW TO STAY CENTERED

People can sometimes stay calm during a conflict when it is pretty clear that things will turn out okay. They may be confident in the outcome because of a powerful position they have. Sometimes a person feels that he or she is holding a trump card. This person may recognize this particular type of conflict or pattern and know that it is survivable and that all will be well in the end. What we will look at in this chapter is how to stay centered—that is, calm and relaxed while being able to make extremely rapid choices about what you will say and do.

Practice and experience are important and helpful when dealing with conflict, but they can come together to help you the most when—in the thick of things—you can calmly make effective choices about what to do.

Beyond the help that practiced strategies, experience, attitude, or even being powerful can give us is the ability to exercise what might be called *controlled relaxation.* Martial artists, yoga practitioners, and others refer to this ability to deliberately relax mind and body together at a moment's notice and without thought as *centering*.

You may be surprised at what you already know about centering.

If you paint or draw, play a musical instrument, ski, golf, or play any sport, you probably already have been centering yourself from time to time. If you can tell a joke well without effort, or dance, or just automatically seem to know what piece to move on a checkerboard, you have probably been centering.

HOW CENTERING HELPS YOU IN A CONFLICT SITUATION

Centering is better than strategizing when you are in a conflict situation. With a strategy, you plan to do or say something based on your expectation of the other person's action—"I'll say 'A,' and he'll say, 'B.' Then I'll say 'Z,' and that'll get him!" Of course, your carefully planned strategy goes right out the window if the other guy says "Z" (or something unexpected, like "LMNOP") before you do.

Centering is a technique that leads to the abandonment of strategy in favor of allowing the appropriate choice of action or relationship with the other person to emerge.

Sound strange?

You have probably heard or read something about "fight or flight." The idea is that our brains tend to react in one of two ways when we are under stress. For example, if we are in a conflict, we can either confront the other person (fight) or walk away and hope nothing else happens (flight). This may have worked pretty well for our ancestors. If you were confronted with a saber-toothed cat, for example, you would quickly either run away or hit it with something, depending on your preferences. Nowadays, when we are faced with a conflict, we can often sense our body getting ready for fight or flight—our muscles tense, our heart pumps a little harder, and we get an adrenaline rush.

This physical fight-or-flight reaction still happens when we are centered. The difference is that when we are centered, we are able to send this energy toward a third choice. Think about it: one choice is to fight, the other choice is to flee. Both can make things worse than they already are. When you are centered, you can calmly apply what you are learning about engaging conflict and make split-second adjustments depending on what will work best for you and the other person.

Like every other technique in this book, centering is a simple approach that can be very effective the more you practice it. The following exercise may be your first step toward staying cool in a conflict.

A SIMPLE CENTERING EXERCISE

Here is how you do it:

You can find your physical center about three inches below your navel. Stand comfortably with your feet about shoulder width apart, take in a deep breath, pulling your shoulders up toward your ears as you do so. Let the breath out and let your shoulders fall as you breathe out. Imagine any muscular tension running like water from every part of your body, down your legs, and out through the soles of your feet into the floor.

There are many tapes with calming music and centering instructions that can help you with this exercise. If it feels a little strange, that's okay—you are learning a new skill. The more often you can intentionally relax, the better you will become at it.

Smile a little smile as you relax. Breathe normally and enjoy the image of stress flowing into the floor through the soles of your feet. For example, if you have some tension in your neck, keep smiling and imagine the tension starting as a slow trickle that runs through your body and out through the soles of your feet and into the floor. Picture it in your mind.

When you feel ready, take the fingertips of one hand and lightly touch your center point—two or three inches below your navel. Breathe in and out: let your belly go in and out like a lung as you breathe. This will help you to feel where your center point is and remember it.

Relax and smile as you continue to breathe. It's funny, but when you pay attention to yourself breathing, it can sometimes be difficult to not make yourself breathe. As you focus on your center, let yourself breathe easily—as naturally as if you were not paying attention to it. Stay focused on your center point—you can keep your hand there if you want—and notice each one of your natural breaths. Each time you breathe in, say quietly to yourself, "Breathe in." As you breathe out, say, "Breathe out."

You won't be perfect as you do this, but enjoy it, continue to breathe, smile, and say, "Breathe in . . . breathe out," with each breath.

Once you get the hang of it, you are ready to begin learning to take this practice into your everyday life. In a conflict situation? Find your center point, breathe, slow down your thinking, and make good choices.

Forgive yourself if you don't do this perfectly, keep practicing, and have fun.

. . . .

For a more detailed relaxation and centering exercise, see *The Conflict Management Skills Workshop* by Bill Withers (AMACOM, 2002).

. . . .

CHAPTER VIII

WAYS TO ENGAGE CONFLICT ON THE JOB—UP, DOWN, AND SIDEWAYS

Although conflict occurs at all levels of organizations, we personally face differences at three levels: bosses, peers, and, if we are in a leadership position, constituents. As mentioned earlier, the real issue is not so much that conflict occurs, but rather how you handle conflict when it does.

Whatever the level, there are four questions you need to consider in determining your approach to the person with whom you have a conflict.

1. Which of the four behavioral styles from Chapter 6 (aggressive, nonassertive, passive-aggressive, or assertive) does this person seem to be using?
2. What is the person's usual method of handling conflict?
3. What might he or she value in this situation?
4. What should your approach be?

In addition to considering how to manage conflict with someone, you should also examine certain measures you can take to work more effectively with others, whatever their level may be.

GOING UP

When it comes to bosses, some are great, most are okay, and a few are really miserable. But whether great, okay, or miserable, the boss is still the boss, and it is to your advantage to accept that fact and work toward resolving conflict when it occurs or toward preventing it from happening in the first place.

When you are in conflict with those above you in the organization, you may feel that you are at the highest level of risk. You may also feel somewhat limited in the approaches that can be taken. For example, it wouldn't normally be considered wise to attempt the competing approach with a boss who is being aggressive. Sometimes, even attempting compromise may be out of the question. Although these approaches may seem risky when approaching a superior, success can depend on how you approach the individual. Consider the following case study:

CASE STUDY

Ed manages a department of thirteen professional staff members. You have worked for him for two years. He has a reputation for being loud, rude, and hard-nosed with most of his employees—you included. In past conflicts, you've tried to argue your point, but to no avail. Because of these disagreements, your relationship seems to have deteriorated.

1. Which of the four behavioral styles from Chapter 6 (aggressive, nonassertive, passive-aggressive, or assertive) does Ed seem to be using?

_____

2. What is his probable method of handling conflict?

_____

_____

_____

_____

3. What values may contribute to his behavior?

_____

_____

_____

_____

4. What would a low-risk approach be if you were to have a difference with Ed? What would be the probable results?

_____

_____

_____

_____

5. What would a high-risk approach be? What would be the probable results?

_____

_____

_____

_____

The next study is the real thing. Choose someone above you in your organization with whom you have experienced conflict.

Name:

1. What is his or her usual method of handling conflict?

_____

_____

_____

_____

2. What does he or she value when involved in conflict?

_____

_____

_____

_____

3. What would a low-risk approach be? What would be the probable results?

_____

_____

_____

_____

4. What would a high-risk approach be? What would be the probable results?

_____

_____

_____

_____

5. Do your answers differ from the way you've handled conflict situations with this person in the past? If so, what will your approach be now?

_____

_____

_____

_____

_____

_____

WORKING MORE EFFECTIVELY WITH BOSSES

As mentioned earlier, you can often prevent conflicts from happening in the first place. It may mean adjustments on your part, but often the cost is small when compared with the potential conflict. We tend to get along better with people who have values similar to our own. A major help in working more effectively with bosses is to adapt your behavior to theirs where you can. This doesn't mean changing your lifestyle, but it does imply a willingness to make certain changes and perhaps a few concessions—in other words, a willingness to use a combination of compromise and accommodation to help build the relationship.

Consider the following questions for working more effectively with your boss:

1. When does your boss arrive? Leave?

_____

2. Does your boss take long or short lunches, frequent or few breaks?

---

3. How neat is your boss's workplace?

---

4. What time of the day is your boss most receptive to you?

---

5. Does your boss prefer written or verbal reports? Concise or detailed?

---

6. Does your boss welcome new ideas or resist them?

---

7. Which of the four behavioral styles from Chapter 6 (aggressive, nonassertive, passive-aggressive, or assertive) does your boss seem to be using?

---

8. How could you change your style accordingly?

When answering these questions, you may discover value differences between yourself and your boss. Ask yourself: "Where can I compromise?" "Where can I accommodate?" "What is it worth to me?" Sometimes, you might think it would be much easier just to be left alone so you can do your job. However, your relationship with your boss (whether you agree with the person or not) always plays a critical role in your success or failure in the workplace.

GOING SIDEWAYS

You may feel more comfortable exploring potential approaches and possible results for managing differences with peers. It might be appropriate to attempt competing if the situation is warranted, or perhaps you can insist on resolving the issue through compromise.

Even though you may have more flexibility when dealing with peers, it is still important to be able to work well with them. This includes not only colleagues in your department but also other departments as well. How you perform your job is important, but how you deal with others is just as important. Consider the following case study:

CASE STUDY

Grace is a newly hired colleague in your department. The two of you were assigned to an interdepartmental team about six weeks ago. Initially, things seemed to be going well. However, two members of the team recently approached you about Grace's concern over some negative comments she said you made regarding the team's direction. The truth is that you like the direction the team is moving in, have never made any negative comments, and enjoy being a member of this group effort. You later approached Grace about this situation, and she appeared offended that you could even think such a thing and denied saying anything to anybody. Then yesterday, your boss called you in to let you know he had heard from a confidential source that the team was concerned about your behavior.

1. Which of the four behavioral styles from Chapter 6 (aggressive, nonassertive, passive-aggressive, or assertive) does Grace seem to be using?

_____

2. What is her probable method of handling conflict?

_____

_____

_____

_____

3. What might she value in this situation?

_____

_____

_____

4. What would be a low-risk approach? What would be the probable results?

_____

_____

_____

_____

5. What would be a high-risk approach? What would be the probable results?

_____

_____

_____

_____

Choose a colleague with whom you have experienced conflict.

Name:

1. Which of the four behavioral styles from Chapter 6 (aggressive, nonassertive, passive-aggressive, or assertive) does this person seem to be using?

_____

2. What is his or her usual method of handling conflict?

_____

_____

_____

_____

_____

3. What might he or she value when involved in conflict?

_____

_____

_____

_____

4. What would be a low-risk approach? What would be the probable results?

_____

_____

_____

_____

5. What would be a high-risk approach? What would be the probable results?

_____

_____

_____

_____

6. Do your answers differ from the way you've engaged in conflict with this person in the past? If so, what will your approach be now?

_____

_____

_____

_____

_____

WORKING MORE EFFECTIVELY WITH PEERS

The ability to work well with your peers is an important characteristic in the workplace. Often, it is a major factor in determining who is chosen for special projects or for promotion.

Consider the following questions when attempting to work more effectively with peers:

1. Do you both respect and understand each other's roles? Briefly describe them.

_____

_____

_____

_____

2. Do you understand each other's tasks? Briefly list them.

_____

_____

_____

_____

3. Are there agreed-to time frames you are both meeting?

_____

_____

_____

_____

4. Is each of you willing to confront and deal with differences?

_____

_____

_____

_____

5. How well do both of you handle compromise?

_____

_____

_____

_____

   If you are currently in conflict with a peer, using the answers to these questions as a starting point for engaging the differences will help. Of course, somebody's got to go first—and you're the one reading this book.

GOING DOWN

As a leader in your company, you gain the power to hold others accountable, but you also become much more accountable for your actions. Fairness becomes a critical factor.

   You are also obligated to help your people to develop to the highest possible level and to appraise their performance and behavior as objectively as you can.

   When you are having differences with an employee, you need to be aware of two possibly conflicting issues: On the one hand, you have complete flexibility in choosing any of the five methods of conflict resolution; on the other hand, you need to be careful not to misuse certain methods. Even though you have the power to force the win/lose outcome, you need to give fair consideration when choosing your approach to the situation. Consider the following case study.

CASE STUDY

You hired Lucille approximately a year ago. She is a very pleas-
ant person, but she has a difficult time accepting any kind of

feedback. Her work performance fluctuates between needing improvement and being acceptable. Each time you've tried to give her constructive criticism, she's become emotional and then withdrawn; so you've recently avoided discussing her job performance.

You have to give her annual performance review in two weeks.

1. Which of the four behavioral styles from Chapter 6 (aggressive, nonassertive, passive-aggressive, or assertive) does Lucille seem to be using?

_____

2. What is her probable method of handling conflict?

_____

_____

_____

_____

3. What might she value in this situation?

_____

_____

_____

_____

4. What would be a low-risk approach to her performance review? What would be the probable results?

_____

_____

_____

_____

5. What would be a high-risk approach? What would be the probable results?

_____

_____

_____

_____

Choose an employee with whom you are currently experiencing conflict.

Name:

1. Which of the four behavioral styles from Chapter 6 (aggressive, nonassertive, passive-aggressive, or assertive) does this person seem to be using?

_____

2. What is his or her usual method of handling conflict?

_____

_____

_____

_____

3. What does he or she value when involved in conflict?

_____

_____

_____

_____

4. What would a low-risk approach be? What would be the probable results?

_____

_____

_____

_____

5. What would a high-risk approach be? What would be the probable results?

_____

_____

_____

_____

6. Do your answers differ from the way you've handled conflict situations with this person in the past? If so, what will your approach be now?

_____

_____

_____

_____

_____

_____

WORKING MORE EFFECTIVELY WITH EMPLOYEES

As with bosses and peers, there are measures you can take to prevent many conflicts from occurring in the first place. The key factor when you manage others is that you are the controlling influence. You set the atmosphere for those you manage.

Consider using the following questions when working with employees:

1. When do you make yourself available to your employees?

_____

_____

2. Do you get back to them when you say you will?

_____

_____

3. What active listening skills do you use? Which skills do you still need to develop?

_____

_____

_____

_____

4. How well do you apply the feedback skills from Chapter 5?

_____

_____

_____

_____

5. What methods do you use to resolve differences with employees?

_____

_____

_____

_____

6. What do you do to help them develop additional skills?

_____

_____

_____

_____

7. What do you do to encourage them to take on more challenging tasks?

_____

_____

_____

_____

8. What do you know about their personal lives?

_____

_____

The more questions you are able to answer positively, the greater the possibility you are establishing a positive atmosphere. You can provide not only an opportunity for growth and success for them and yourself but also help to prevent the possibility of unnecessary grievances or other legal problems for your company.

In short, if the atmosphere is positive, conflicts will be minimized. And if the atmosphere is negative, you should expect not only the worst but also accept the responsibility for having created it through poor management.

9

CHAPTER IX

WAYS TO WORK WITH TEAMS
IN CONFLICT

The great contradiction about teams is that we want the people on them to get along, but we have teams so that we can get a variety of ways of looking at things. The key to team building is not to get everyone to agree all of the time but to figure out how people can disagree, use their differing points of view to create new approaches and ideas, and then implement those new approaches and ideas. As management thinker Tom Peters said, "If two people in business always agree, then one of them is unnecessary."

An easy mistake to make is to think of the team as a single mind or personality. Even if a team is performing very well, conflicts will necessarily arise. Creatively and positively engaging in conflict becomes the true work of the team.

Questions About Your Team

1. What is your current role: member? leader?
2. What tasks are you personally responsible for?
3. Are you personally involved in a conflict with another team member? Considering the information in this book, what could you do to manage the situation?
4. What other conflicts exist within the team?
5. What needs to be done?
6. Are there any members who don't want to "play"? Describe.
7. What do you think the team should do?
8. How does the team leader interact with the team?

SOME BASICS OF TEAM BUILDING AND CONFLICT

Too often, differences in team meetings are simply smoothed over by the leader or other members. Of course, in these cases the conflict doesn't dissipate, it just simmers until a later date. This form of conflict avoidance can lead to the gradual buildup of resentment among team members. Because engaging in conflict is a necessary part of high-performance team building, you need to consider the relationship between team building and conflict.

DECISION MAKING: VOTING VS. CONSENSUS

When teams are allowed to make their own decisions, there are three possibilities: voting, consensus, or direction.

1. *Voting.* Voting is an effective way to move decisions forward, but it is a win/lose solution and can promote division within the team.
2. *Consensus.* Reaching consensus is more difficult than voting, but it is the preferred approach to team-based decisions. It does, of course, take longer, and differences will occur in the process. However, in the end, everyone supports the final decision.
3. *Direction.* It is often necessary and appropriate for the leader of the team to make a decision and direct the team about the issue at hand.

No matter which of these approaches is used, the key is to be clear ahead of time about what options are available and allowed and what approach will be used.

MEMBERSHIP

Being a member of a team is not easy for many of us, especially if we're accustomed to making decisions on our own. When you become a team player, you enter into an interdependent relationship. You may even feel that you are giving up your individuality, but in a very real sense you are making an individual contribution to a group effort that usually produces a greater end result than you could have achieved on your own.

Consider the following elements of team membership dynamics:

■ *Participation.* As a team member, you are expected to participate in a balanced manner, that is, to not be dominant or withdrawn, while at the same time helping others to maintain their own balance.

■ *Selling.* You probably feel your ideas are great. Sometimes they are. Your responsibility as a team member is to prepare ahead of time and to present your ideas in a way that shows the team the value acting on these ideas will add. You also need to be able to know when to compromise: letting go of ownership of an idea, accepting elements of other ideas to add to your own, or allowing your idea to be substituted for by another, better one.

■ *Relinquishing.* This is the big one. What if you sell to the best of your ability, but the team won't buy? Some team members temporarily withdraw. Some don't want to play anymore . . . ever. This is the point where the rest of the team discovers what kind of team player you really are. Your responsibility at this point is to relinquish your position. Not only do you need to give it up, you must also be willing to support and even defend the team's direction.

■ *Evaluating.* Effective teams are constantly reviewing their performance: What worked? What could have been done better? How could it be done differently next time? Team members need to become good at giving and receiving feedback (see Chapter 5) in order to learn from mistakes and successes and to apply that learning to the team's future work together.

■ *Relationship.* As a team member, you are responsible for your relationship with other team members. If there is a personal conflict, it is up to you to help resolve it. Personal conflicts in team efforts fracture and sometimes prevent task accomplishment.

■ *Task Accomplishment.* When acting as a team member, it is critical that you are clear on your task responsibility. This includes what you have to do, when it has to be completed, and any steps in between. In an interdependent relationship, one member's failure can trigger the delay of other people's efforts and affect the outcome of the entire team. Being a good team player isn't easy. Bringing excess baggage, using hidden agendas, or protecting authorship of personal ideas all serve to prevent the overall direction. You can better serve yourself and the other members if you focus on what is best for the team rather than for yourself.

LEADERSHIP

Another area where companies have failed to provide good orientation regarding team building is in leadership. Sometimes groups are simply told, "Go be a team, make consensus decisions, and, by the way, everybody's equal." Well, everyone may be equal, but newly formed teams need leaders, and even sophisticated teams need facilitators to keep things moving.

Leaders can be appointed or elected, but in the beginning, *someone* must be in control. Author and consultant Peter Block has said that we can all be partners and still have a "partner in charge." Leadership has certain responsibilities that are different from those of membership. Consider the following list of leadership requirements:

■ *Engaging Conflict.* If team members fail to resolve issues themselves, it is the leader's responsibility to surface the issues so that they can be constructively engaged. Sometimes, this is best done privately, but sometimes it may be better to involve the team as a whole.

■ *Working with Uncooperative Members.* If there is an individual on the team who is aggressive in team interaction, it may be up to the team leader to talk to the individual regarding his or her behavior. In severe situations, this may even include asking the member to leave the team. Anyone can be replaced, so it is unfair for the team to be held back because of one individual.

■ *Drawing Out Unassertive Members.* Some team members may have difficulty speaking out in a group. In this case, the team leader has two issues to deal with: getting the member's ideas outside the team setting and encouraging the individual to be more assertive in his or her interaction within the team setting.

■ *Conducting Productive Meetings.* There are two types of meetings: productive and ridiculous. If you are having a meeting to talk about something everyone already knows about or agrees to, you are wasting your time. The following hints can help to produce more productive meetings:

- Have an agenda in advance, with time limits for each item.
- Start on time.
- Stay on track.
- End with everyone knowing his or her specific assignments and timetables.
- End on time.
- Send minutes to team members within two days following each meeting.
- If nothing new is going to happen at or because of the meeting, don't have it.

■ *Remaining Objective.* Team leaders must be objective enough to manage both tasks and relationships. They need to be involved as a functioning member while also being able to extricate themselves so that they can observe both group dynamics and task progress.

Leading a team requires an individual who wants the position, is capable of directing task accomplishment, and has an understanding of the dynamics involved in a group effort.

Team building requires the efforts of everyone involved. Companies need to be willing to provide the necessary training to get their teams off to a good start. Without proper training, an organization will flounder in conflict, unresolved differences, and failed tasks. However, if the proper orientation is provided, a lot can be accomplished.

Think of a team you are on and ask yourself the following questions:

1. Is the purpose of the team clear?

_____

2. How well do people understand what is expected of them?

_____

_____

_____

_____

3. Would better answers to the previous two questions help to eliminate unnecessary conflict?

_____

_____

_____

_____

4. How can you use what you are learning about conflict to make your team more effective?

_____

_____

_____

_____

CHAPTER X

10

CAN ALL THIS CONFLICT
BE GOOD FOR ME?

A helpful thing to know about yourself in a conflict situation is how you feel about conflict in general. You have had a chance in this book to answer some questions about conflicts you are engaged in, how you may approach conflict, how to give and get feedback, how you listen, and how you can engage in conflict with your coworkers.

Now you can answer the important question about whether conflict can have positive value. Is it something to avoid at all costs, is it something to seek out, or is conflict something somewhere in between?

Think of a specific conflict situation at work that you have been a part of, will be a part of, should be a part of, or would like to be a part of. Then answer these final questions, which we have borrowed from *The Conflict Management Skills Workshop* by Bill Withers.

WIIFM? (What's in it for me?)

- What might I gain by being a part of this conflict?
- What might I learn by being a part of this conflict?
- What might change about me as a result of being a part of this conflict?

WIIFOP? (What's in it for the other person?)

- What might the other person(s) gain because I am a part of this conflict?

WIIFU? (What's in it for us?)

- What might everyone involved gain because I am a part of this conflict?
- What might my team or department and I gain because I am a part of this conflict?
- What might the company gain because I am a part of this conflict?

■ Can groups of people (teams, departments, or companies) learn from conflict? If they can, what can they learn?

So, if there are benefits to conflict, should you wait for conflict to come to the surface all by itself, or should you look for hidden conflict and bring it up on purpose? What would you do if you decide to constructively leave conflict alone? What would you do if you decide to constructively bring conflict to the surface?

CHAPTER XI

WHY DO I CARE?

I was sitting in the cafeteria listening to a colleague go on about her horrible day. Her morning had begun with a phone argument between her and her ex-husband that had somehow spilled over into an argument with her current husband. Then, she went outside to find her car blocked by the neighbor's trash cans. Later, someone cut her off in traffic. She received a work assignment that she considered a waste of time, and the book she was reading for a class she was taking was stupid.

I looked at her over my juice box and thought, "You gotta get a shorter list of things that make you mad."

Something to consider when thinking about conflict at work is whether what you are fighting about is worth the fight. Pediatrician Marvin Gersh, in his very funny and wise book *How to Raise Children at Home in Your Spare Time*, tells of two parents who were concerned about whether it was better for their child to sleep with the bedroom door open or closed. They took this problem to the doctor who reminded them that the open or closed door decision was not exactly a moral question.

A good question to think about before engaging in conflict with another person is: "Why does this matter so much to me?" Asking this question isn't about being lazy or cowardly; it is a question that can help us to decide whether we are fighting out of habit or tradition, or whether this is a difference worth engaging.

Borrow a page from process improvement and root cause analysis to ask yourself *why* five times.

"This really makes me mad!"

Why?

"Because I should get the new style of computer monitor that the other managers are getting."

Why do I care?

"Because I'm the only manager who doesn't have one and it makes me look bad."

Why does it make me look bad? Or, *why do I care about this?*

. . . and so on. As the manager from our example drills down into the cause of her concern by asking *why* five times, she may discover that it is important to assert herself to get the new computer monitor or may just as well discover that it is not important.

If the difference in question is worth engaging, having asked ourselves *why* five times will help us to clarify our position and its importance. We will also have learned about what matters to us as we edit the list of things that we are willing to stand up for.

The manager in our example says that not having the new type of computer monitor makes her look bad. Nobody wants to look bad, so it may seem reasonable to be angry about not having the new monitor. As we continue to ask why, we may get to a deeper issue:

Why does it make me look bad? Or, *why do I care about this?*

"The new monitor was distributed to all managers, and people are talking about them as if they are a perk. If I don't have one, then I don't have the perk that all of the other managers are getting, and it sends me and others the message that I am not as important."

See how quickly asking *why* gets us into an analysis of what matters? In this case, the manager is finding out or acknowledging that she considers the new monitor to be a sort of badge of her rank and an indication of her relative worth. The next why question could go in several directions, and our manager may need to try a few in order to get to the core of what is bothering her.

Why do I care what others think? Or, *why do I think that the monitors are a symbol of being a manager?* Or, *why do I think that I would be left off the new monitor list?*

By the time we get to the fifth *why*, the examination of the issue is getting close to what may really be bothering us. Our manager in the example will now have to challenge herself to honestly investigate a little of what makes her tick. She may decide that this is something worth pursuing or something to be left alone. She may also find that there is something more important to work on— either by herself or with others in her company.

Five is not a magic number, but it is a good guideline. Five *why*s will usually get us to a point where we begin to really need to think about what matters. Depending on the issue and how we ask and answer the question, you may get there in four, or it may take more than five. When I am working with someone and asking *why* five times, the person usually starts to get annoyed by about the fourth why. You may find that that is the case when you do the exercise by yourself. It often means that your analysis is getting somewhere.

Try this exercise: Think of a conflict you are engaged in. Begin by asking yourself, "What do I want?" Then ask yourself, "Why?" Be strict with yourself, and challenge your answer by asking *why* again, then ask *why* about that answer, and so on. Write your five answers out to be sure that you are taking the time to truly think this through.

Each time you answer the question *why*, refine your answer and dig a little deeper into what matters to you. If my friend in the cafeteria had worked through her list by asking *why* five times, three things may have happened for her. First, she would have had to calm down enough to give her issues some thought. She would also have begun to refine what really matters to her and what does not. Finally, if she identified differences that she chose to engage, she would have thought through the beginnings of an intelligent message she could send to the other person about what she wants and why it is important.

Describe a difference that is on your mind:

_____

_____

_____

_____

_____

_____

1. What would you like to happen if this conflict were positively engaged with the other person?

_____

_____

_____

2. Why does that matter to you?

_____

_____

_____

_____

3. Now continue to ask *why* four more times, and write your answers here.

_____

_____

_____

_____

_____

_____

_____

_____

_____

_____

_____

_____

APPENDIX

BE PREPARED

One of the great gifts of experiencing conflict is that it requires us to think about what matters. One helpful way of applying the reflection questions in this book to a specific situation is to organize them so that they paint a picture of what is going on, what you are thinking and feeling, and what you want to do—including who, what, where, why, and how.

Use the templates on the following pages to organize your thoughts.

I.   Who?

1. With whom are you currently experiencing differences at work?
    Boss(es)/upper management?

    _____

    _____

    Peers?

    _____

    _____

    Employees?

    _____

    _____

2. What core value might the other person have that is influencing his or her choices?

    _____

    _____

    _____

    _____

3. Which of the four behavioral styles from Chapter 6 does this person seem to be using?

    Aggressive
    Nonassertive
    Passive-Aggressive
    Assertive

4. What is his or her usual method of handling conflict?

    _____

    _____

_____

_____

5. What does he or she value when involved in conflict?

_____

_____

_____

_____

6. Who else is involved in or affected by the conflict?

_____

_____

_____

_____

7. Does having these people involved escalate the issue?

_____

_____

_____

_____

8. What values do these people possess that may be in conflict?

_____

_____

_____

_____

II.   What?

1. Write a brief description or story about what is going on.

_____

_____

_____

_____

_____

_____

Is this description objective? If not, try to describe it objectively.

_____

_____

_____

_____

_____

_____

2. What do you want to be different because you have en-
    gaged in this conflict?

_____

_____

_____

_____

3. What is the ideal outcome?

_____

_____

_____

_____

III. When?

    1. Can you plan and agree to a time to talk to the other person that will suit you both?

    _____

    2. Will a certain time make your meeting more likely to be effective than some other time?

    _____

    3. Will all the interested/affected parties be able to make this time?

    _____

    4. Is it better to deal with the conflict when it is happening, immediately afterward, or after a period of time has passed and things have cooled down?

    _____

IV. Where?

    1. Have you chosen a neutral setting or a setting that will lend itself to putting the other person at ease?

    _____

    2. Can you arrange to have other neutral parties there to temper the environment?

    _____

    _____

    _____

    _____

    3. Will having an authority figure there calm the other person or escalate the issue?

    _____

    _____

    _____

    _____

    4. How can you minimize the distractions in the environment?

    _____

    _____

    _____

    _____

V.   Why?

    1. WIIFM? (What's in it for me?)

        a. What might I gain by being a part of this conflict?

_____

_____

_____

_____

_____

        b. What might I learn by being a part of this conflict?

_____

_____

_____

_____

_____

        c. What might change about me as a result of being a part
           of this conflict?

_____

_____

_____

_____

_____

    2. WIIFOP? (What's in it for the other person?)

        a. What might the other person(s) gain because I am a part
           of this conflict?

_____

_____

_____

_____

_____

b. What might they learn?

_____

_____

_____

_____

_____

c. What might change about our relationship?

_____

_____

_____

_____

_____

3. WIIFU? (What's in it for us?)

   a. What might everyone involved gain because I am a part of this conflict?

_____

_____

_____

_____

_____

   b. What might my team or department and I gain because I am a part of this conflict?

_____

_____

_____

_____

_____

c. What might the company gain because I am a part of this
conflict?

_____

_____

_____

_____

_____

4. What would you like to happen if this conflict were positively engaged with the other person?

_____

_____

_____

_____

5. Why does that matter to you?

_____

_____

_____

_____

6. Now continue to ask *why* four more times and write your
answers on this page.

_____

_____

_____

_____

_____

_____

VI. How?

1. Will it be most effective to approach this conflict as a contest to win, as a problem to solve, or as a learning opportunity?

   _____

2. How will you prepare yourself to listen well?

   _____

   _____

   _____

   _____

3. How will you remind yourself to stay cool and listen well while you are in your meeting?

   _____

   _____

   _____

   _____

4. Do your answers differ from the way you've handled conflicting situations with this person in the past? If so, what will your approach be now?

   _____

   _____

   _____

   _____

VII. Communication

Now that you have planned how you'd like to handle the conflict, it's important to come up with some ways to express your point of view.

Use the space below to plan how you will communicate the conflict effectively.

1. At times I feel _____.

_____

_____

_____

_____

2. When you _____, I feel _____.

_____

_____

_____

_____

3. This bothers me because I value _____.

_____

_____

_____

_____

4. How am I helping to cause this problem?

_____

_____

_____

_____

5. How can I help so this does not happen in the future?

_____

_____

_____

_____

6. How would you like to see this be resolved?

_____

_____

_____

_____

FURTHER READING

There are many books to choose from that can help you to keep thinking about conflict on the job. This short list can be a springboard to other reading or—better yet—to your trying some new ideas and actions on for size.

The best first book for learning about negotiation is still *Getting to Yes: Negotiating Agreement Without Giving In* by Roger Fisher, William Ury, and Bruce Patton. It is direct and to the point, and it is a very good how-to manual for what we call *assertive behavior* in this book.

Jay Rothman's book *Resolving Identity-Based Conflict in Nations, Organizations, and Communities* digs into the role that identity plays in seemingly impossible conflicts and makes practical suggestions for engagement.

This book is designed to help you to think about conflict in new ways and to help you be ready as you engage in a difference with another person. Many of the skills we need when we come to the table are parallel to those that are used by mediators. The following resources can help you to learn about mediation and give you new ways to approach others:

- Jennifer E. Beer's *The Mediator's Handbook* is used as a training text by mediators around the world. It is a handy book to reach for when preparing for any difficult conversation.

- *The Promise of Mediation: Responding to Conflict Through Empowerment and Recognition* by Robert A. Baruch Bush and Joseph P. Folger offers ideas to help us to shift our thinking about conflict from a contest to be won to an opportunity for learning.

- The website www.mediation.com has monthly articles by and for people interested in mediation.

How we think about work and our coworkers plays a big part in how we think about and engage in workplace conflict. Still fresh after nearly fifty years is Douglas McGregor's landmark book *The Human Side of Enterprise*. This book is a good reminder for us to check to see if the actions we choose—especially as managers—are consistent with what our beliefs are. As you read this book, you will recognize a lot of the thinking that has become a part of the ideal of how best to work with others. As Warren Bennis wrote in his foreword to the twenty-fifth-anniversary printing, "Much of the work that goes on now could not have happened if this book hadn't been written."

When I am asked what one book people should read about work, the answer has for many years been *The Fifth Discipline: The Art and Practice of the Learning Organization* by Peter Senge. The book is packed with sometimes daunting ideas. If you aren't quite ready to jump into the whole work, start with the fourth chapter, "The Laws of the Fifth Discipline," then flip to the index, look up "dialogue," and read those entries. If what you find there makes sense to you, think about what else you need to learn to be able to apply it to your work.

Finally, think of yourself when you are at your best. What do you do that works for you and the others with whom you come in contact? Make a list and carry it around for a few days. Add to it. Think about it. Live with it. Then take out another piece of paper, set it beside your list, and write down what new things you can do to be at your best at all times.

Have fun.

INDEX